The Joy of Handel and t' 'Messiah'

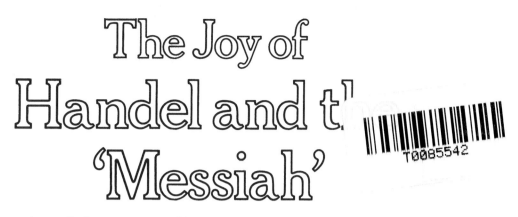

**A graded repertory of his easier keyboard works and best-loved selections from his immortal oratorios.
Selected and arranged by Denes Agay and Frank Metis.**

Order No. YK 21826
US International Standard Book Number: 0.8256.8101.4
UK International Standard Book Number: 0.7119.6760.1

Exclusive Distributors:
Music Sales Corporation
257 Park Avenue South, New York, NY 10010 USA
Music Sales Limited
8/9 Frith Street, London W1V 5TZ England
Music Sales Pty. Limited
120 Rothschild Street, Rosebery, Sydney, NSW 2018, Australia

Printed in the United States of America by
Vicks Lithograph and Printing Corporation

Yorktown Music Press, Inc.
New York/London/Sydney

Foreword

George Frideric Handel (1685–1759), with J.S. Bach the greatest name in baroque music, was a cosmopolitan master whose international success and fame were unsurpassed in his time. His blending of German, Italian, and French influences resulted in a style rarely equaled for sheer vitality and expressiveness. Haydn said of him: "He is the master of us all" and Beethoven thought he was the greatest composer that ever lived. He was also a foremost harpsichordist and organist during his lifetime.

Handel's fame as a composer was due mainly to his operas, oratorios, and festive outdoor music, which to a large extent still occupy a respectable niche in the standard of repertory. "Messiah," of course, is an exceptional item even in this stellar list of masterpieces. This best-loved and most-performed oratorio was written by Handel in twenty-four days during the year 1741. The first performance took place in Dublin, Ireland in 1742. After this first presentation, Handel revised and rewrote much of the score and it was published after his death in 1767. The secret of this works' lasting effect has been well and profusely documented. In it, Handel combined deep religiosity with an unfailing dramatic instinct, so that the audience has not only an uplifting spiritual experience but also participates in a thrilling musical, indeed, theatrical event.

The core and summit of Handel's keyboard output are the sixteen harpsichord suites which, although somewhat neglected today, should be placed next to Bach's Suites and Partitas in the baroque pantheon. His easier keyboard works, of which this volume presents a representative sampling, were written early in his career, most likely before 1720. Their lightness of character, their melodic appeal, and a less than rigorous polyphonic texture give an interesting foretaste of the later "gallant" style and are somewhat closer to the manner of Telemann, than that of J.S. Bach. For all these reasons they are ideal preparatory material to the study of Bach's inventions and polyphonic playing in general.

We hope that pianists and listeners alike can, through this volume, participate in "The Joy of Handel and the Messiah."

Contents

Gavotte

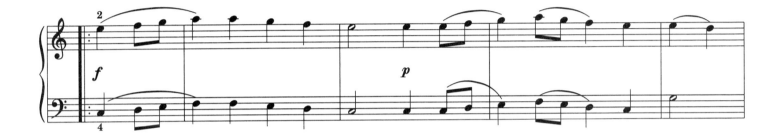

Passepied

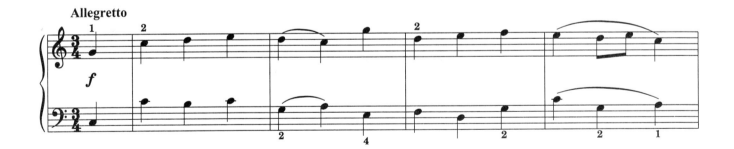

Menuett

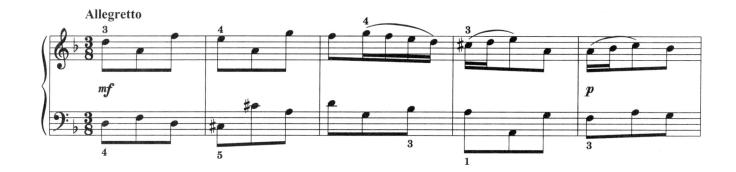

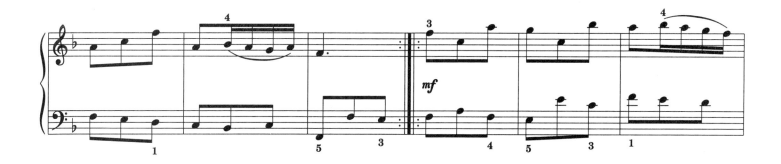

Gavotte

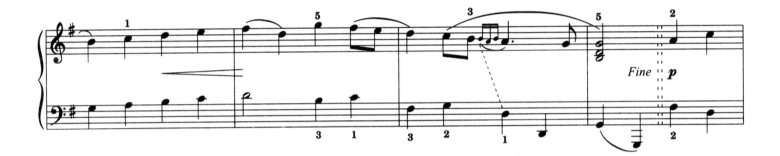

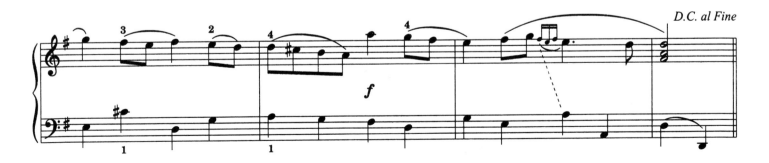

Rigaudon

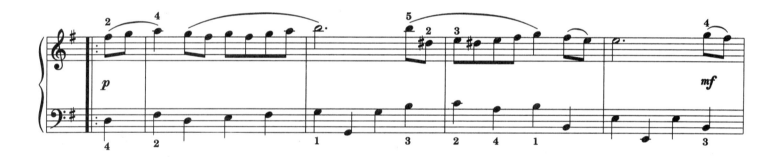

Menuett

"Impertinence"

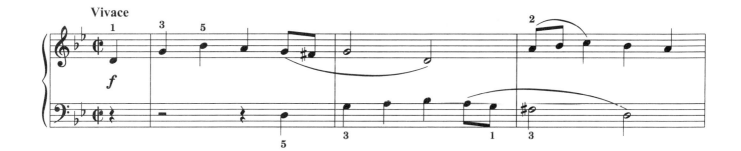

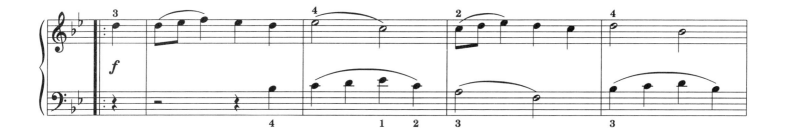

Saraband

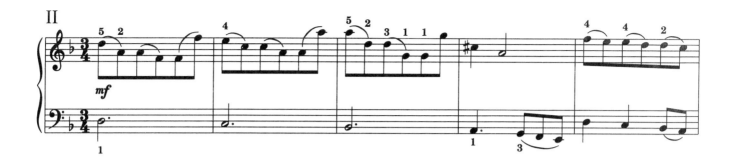

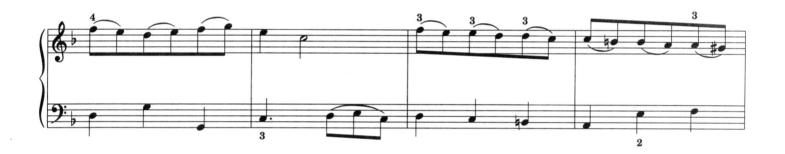

Air und Double

Bourrée

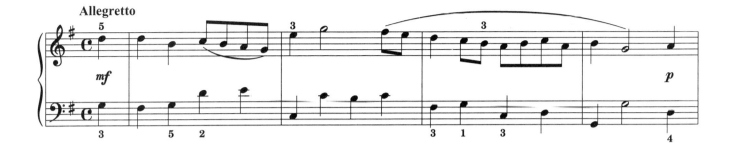

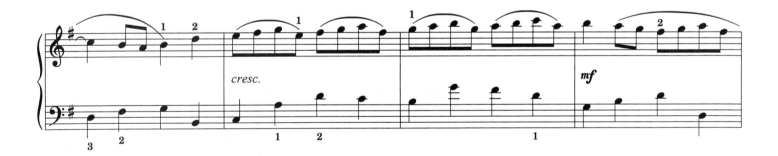

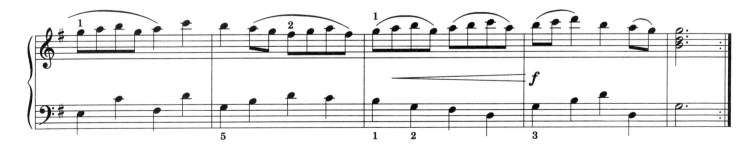

Chaconne
Theme and Six Variations

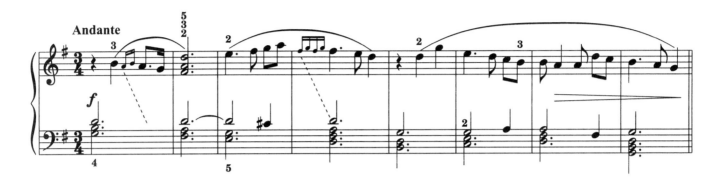

Var. I
Poco più mosso

Var. II

Var. III

Var. IV

Var. V

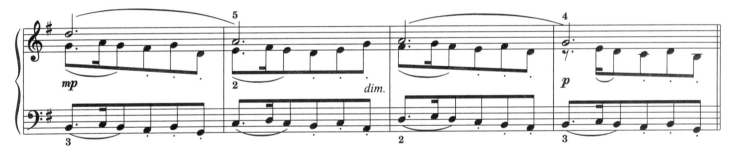

Var. VI

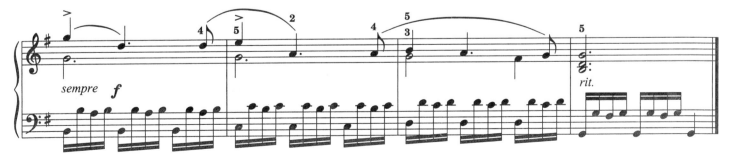

Invention

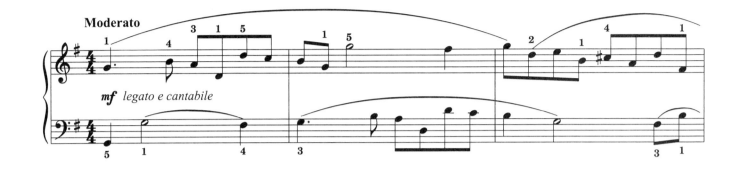

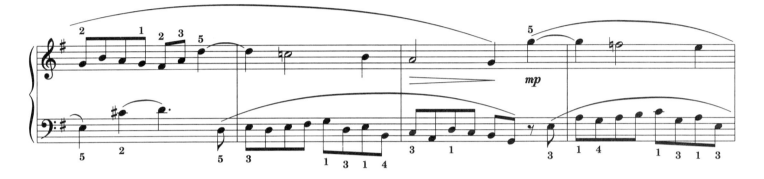

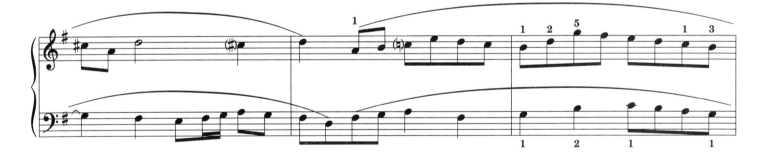

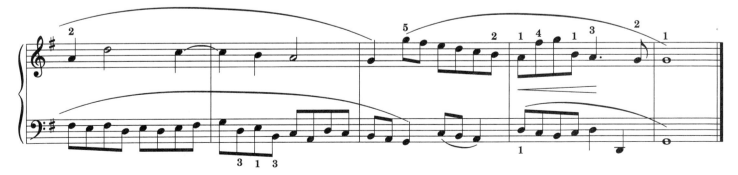

Courante

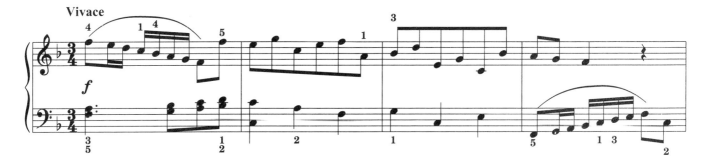

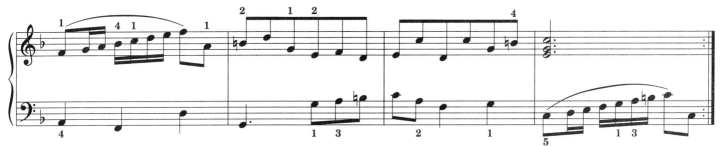

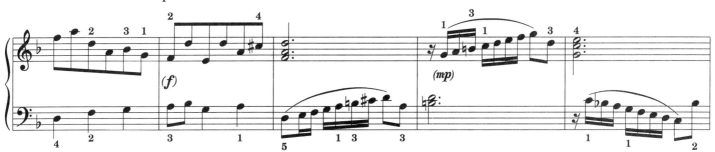

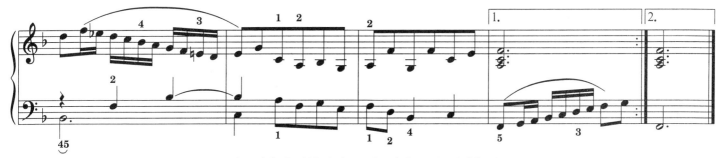

Canzone

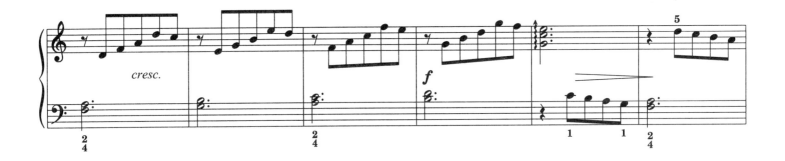

Intrada

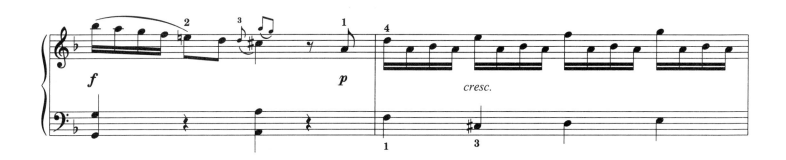

Gigue

Sonatina

Fantasia

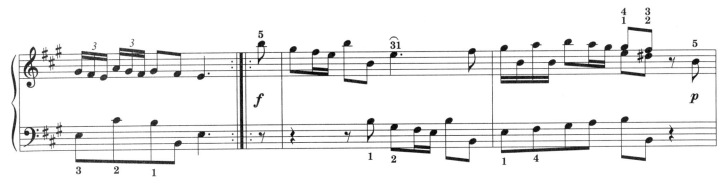

Air and Variations

from Suite No. 1. Book 2

Variation 2

28

Variation 3

Allegro

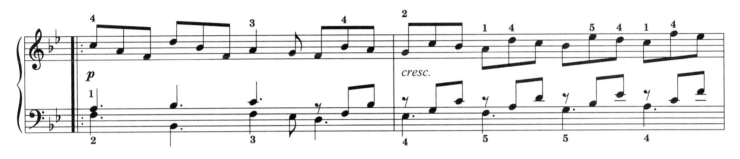

Variation 4

Più mosso

Variation 5

Presto

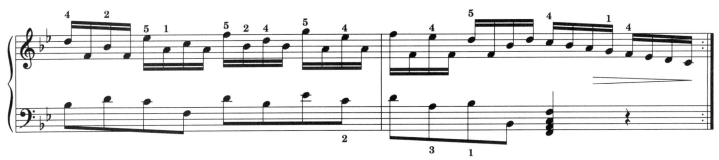

Comfort Ye

from "Messiah"

Arr. by Frank Metis

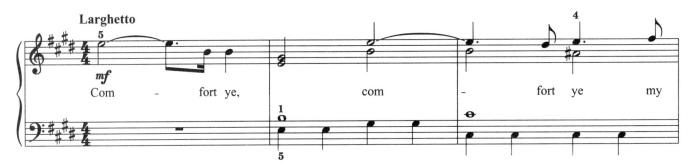

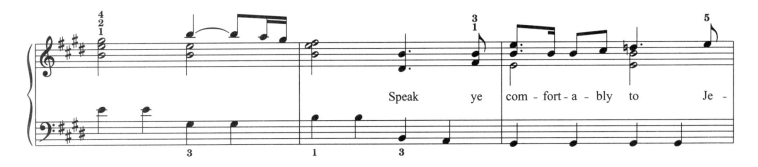

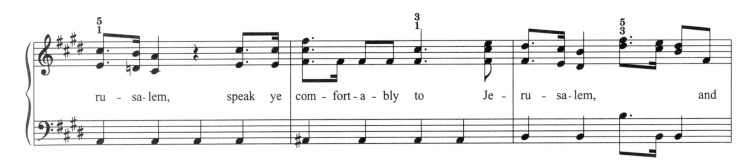

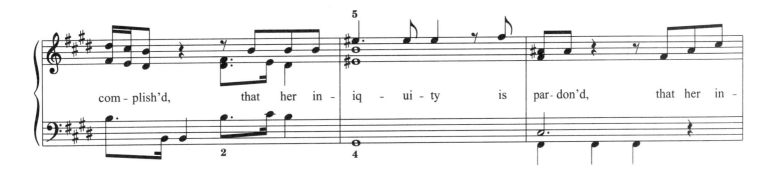

com - plish'd, that her in - iq - ui - ty is par- don'd, that her in -

iq - ui - ty is par - don'd.

The voice of him that crieth in the

wil - der-ness, Pre - pare ye the way of the Lord, make

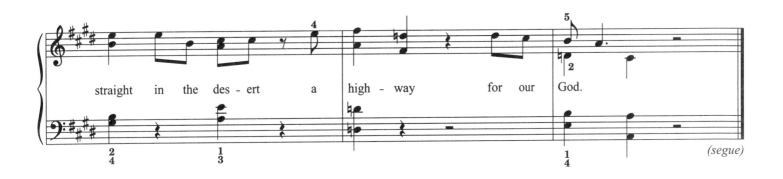

straight in the des - ert a high - way for our God.

(segue)

Ev'ry Valley Shall Be Exalted

from "Messiah"

Arr. by Frank Metis

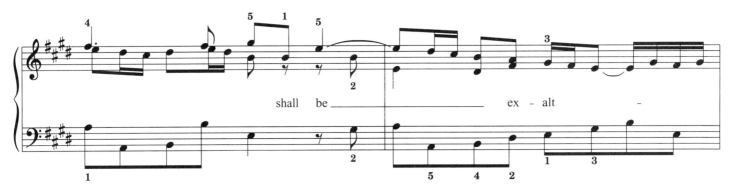

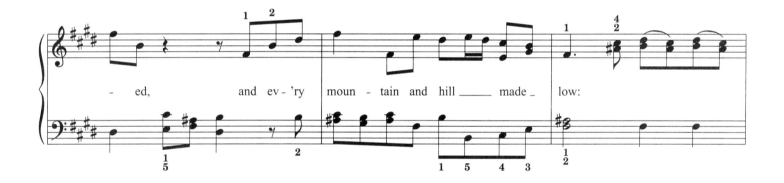

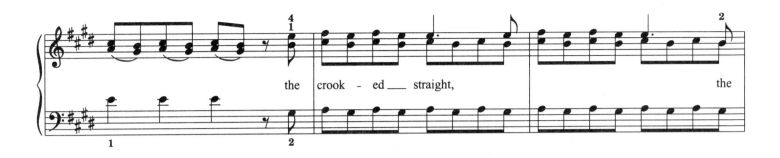

the crook - ed __ straight, the

crook - ed straight, the crook - ed straight, and the rough plac - es plain, _____

_____ and the rough plac - es plain, and the rough plac - es plain, _____

the crook - ed straight, and the rough

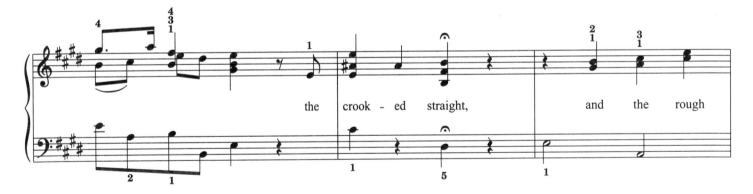

plac - es plain.

And the Glory of the Lord

from "Messiah"

Arr. by Frank Metis

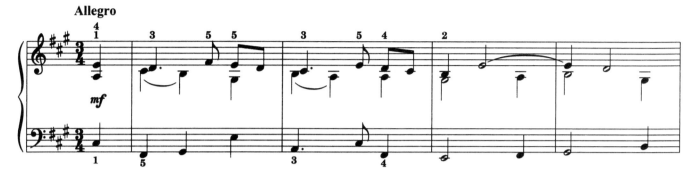

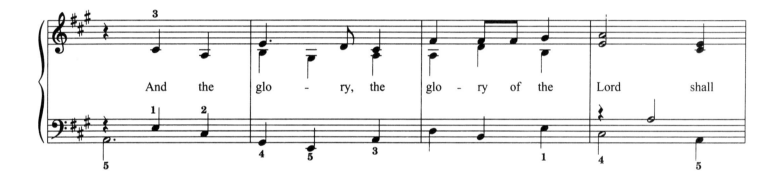

And the glo — ry, the glo — ry of the Lord shall

be re — veal — ed.

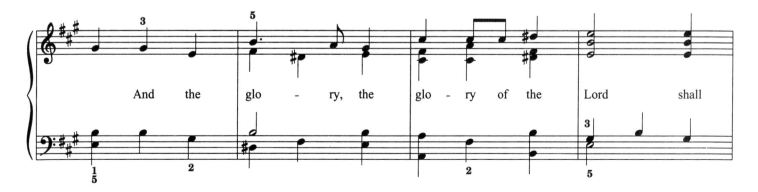

And the glo — ry, the glo — ry of the Lord shall

be re - veal - - ed.

And the glo - ry, the glo - ry of the Lord shall be

f

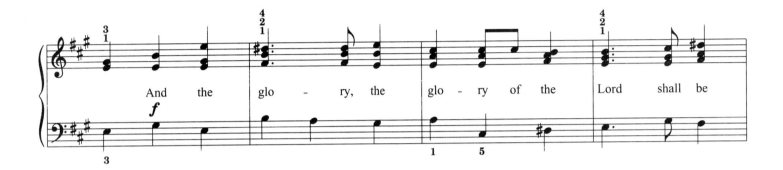

re - veal - ed.

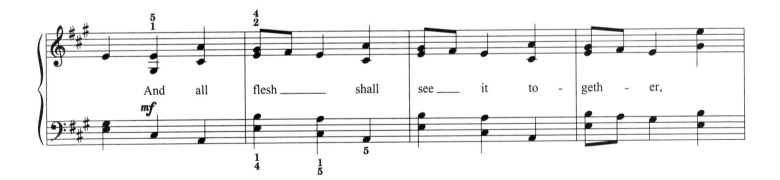

And all flesh ____ shall see ____ it to - geth - er,

mf

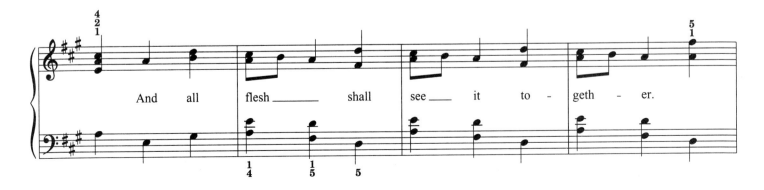

And all flesh ____ shall see ____ it to - geth - er.

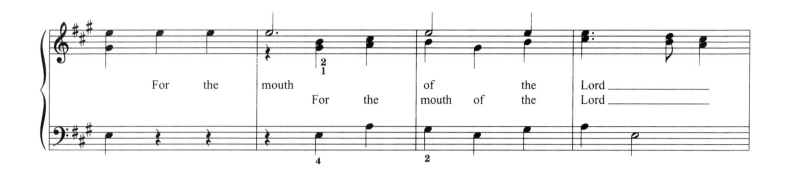

For the mouth of the Lord

For the mouth of the Lord

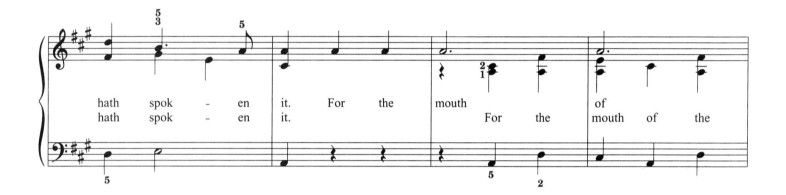

hath spok — en it. For the mouth of

hath spok — en it. For the mouth of the

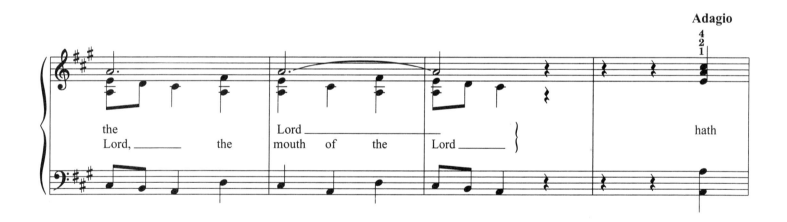

Adagio

the Lord the mouth of the Lord hath

Lord, the mouth of the Lord hath

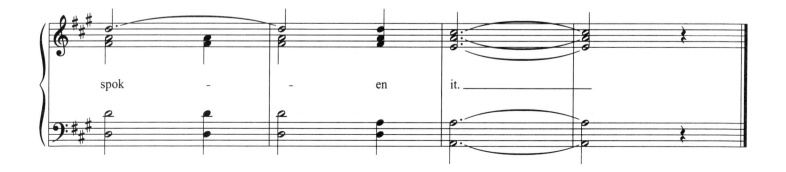

spok — — en it.

O Thou that Tellest Good Tidings to Zion

from "Messiah"

Arr. by Frank Metis

rise, say un - to the cit - ies of Ju - dah, Be - hold your

God! Be - hold, the

glo - ry of _____ the Lord _____ is

ris - en up - on thee, O thou that tell - est good

ti - dings to Zi - on, say un - to the cit - ies of Ju - dah, be -

hold, be - hold, _____ the

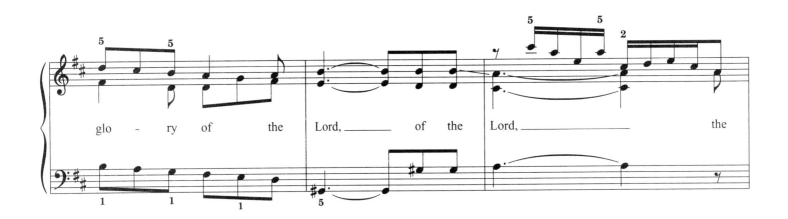

glo - ry of the Lord, _____ of the Lord, _____ the

glo - ry of, ____ the glo - ry of the Lord _____ is

ris - en up - on thee.

ritard.

Pastoral Symphony

from "Messiah"

Arr. by Denes Agay

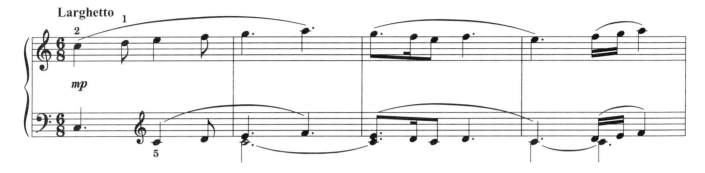

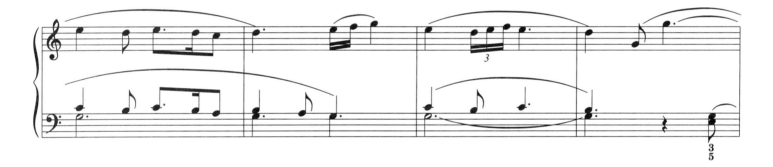

The People that Walked in Darkness

from "Messiah"

Arr. by Frank Metis

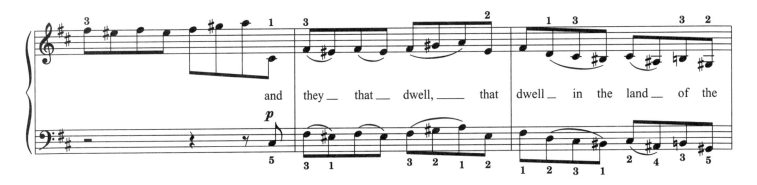

shad - - ow of death, and they _____ that dwell, _____ that

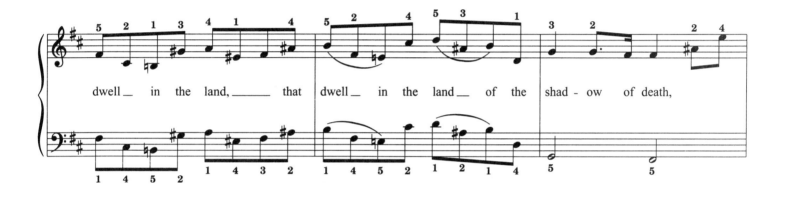

dwell ___ in the land, _____ that dwell ___ in the land ___ of the shad - ow of death,

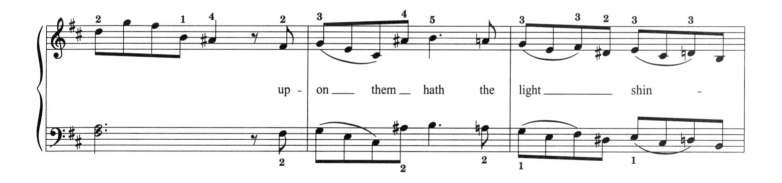

up - on ___ them ___ hath the light _____ shin -

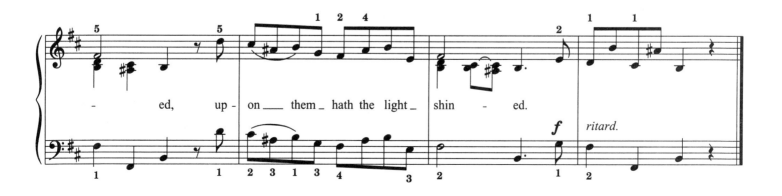

- ed, up - on ___ them ___ hath the light ___ shin - ed.

f   *ritard.*

For Unto Us a Child is Born

from "Messiah"

Arr. by Frank Metis

be up-on his shoul - der, and the gov-ern-ment shall

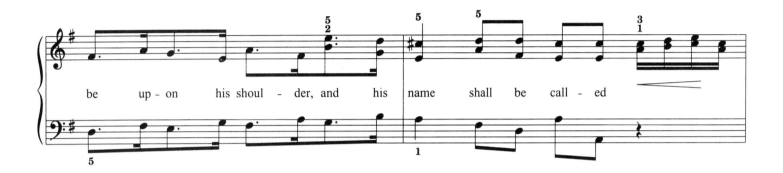

be up-on his shoul - der, and his name shall be call - ed

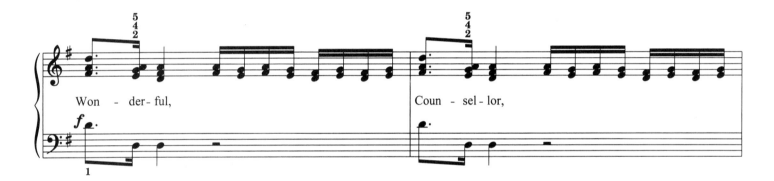

Won - der- ful, Coun - sel - lor,

The might - y God, The ev - er - last - ing Fa - ther, The

Prince of Peace. Won- der- ful, Coun - sel- lor,

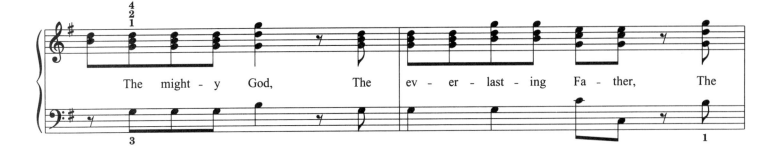

The might-y God, The ev-er-last-ing Fa-ther, The

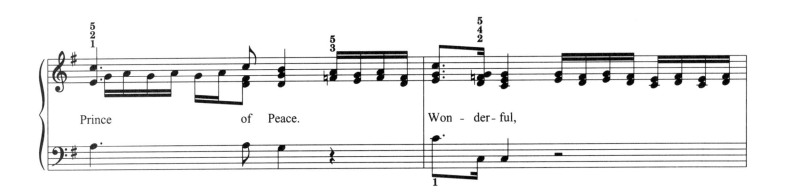

Prince of Peace. Won-der-ful,

Coun-sel-or. The might-y God, The

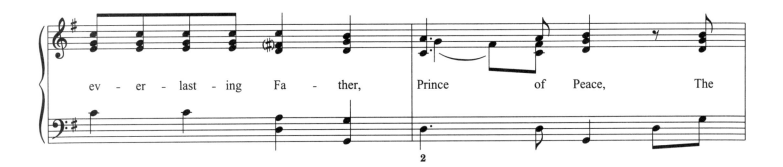

ev-er-last-ing Fa-ther, Prince of Peace, The

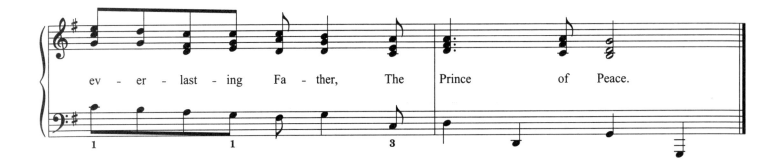

ev-er-last-ing Fa-ther, The Prince of Peace.

Glory to God

from "Messiah"

Arr. by Frank Metis

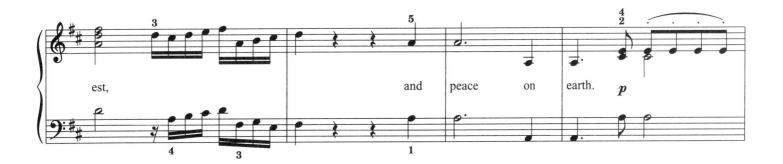

and peace on earth, *p*

mf good will, good will _____ to - ward, good will _____ to - ward

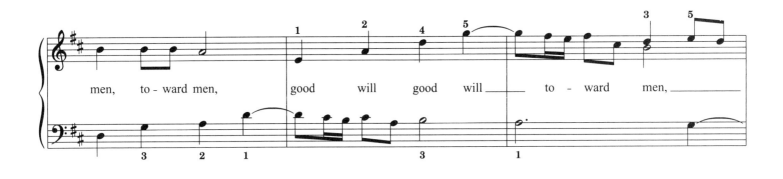

men, to - ward men, good will good will _____ to - ward men, _____

_____ to - ward men. _____ Glory to God, *f*

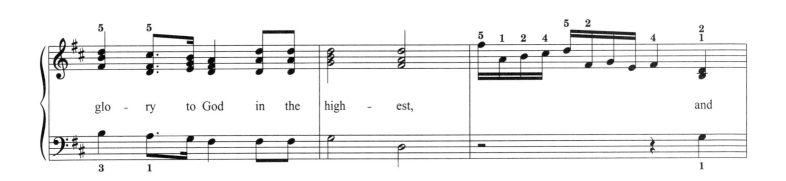

glo - ry to God in the high - est, and

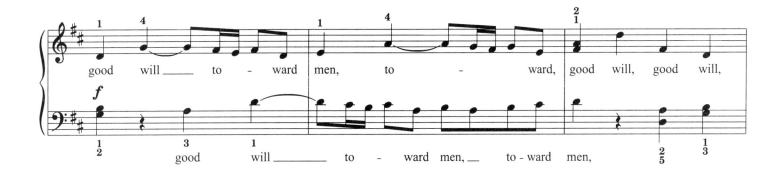

peace on earth, *p*

good will _____ to - ward men, to - ward, good will, good will,

good will _____ to - ward men, _ to - ward men,

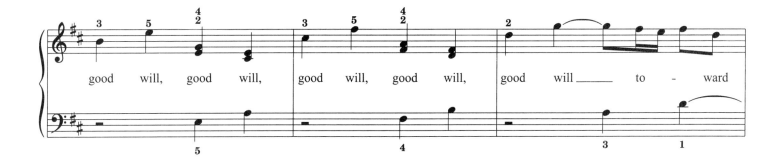

good will, good will, good will, good will, good will _____ to - ward

men, _____ good will _____ to - ward

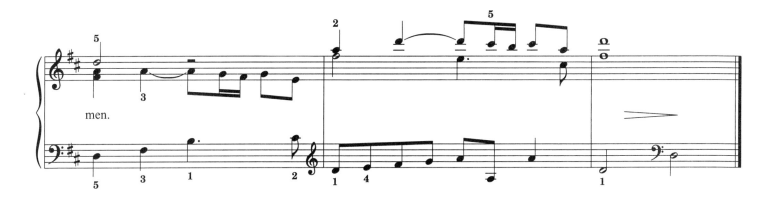

men.

He Shall Feed His Flock

from "Messiah"

Arr. by Denes Agay

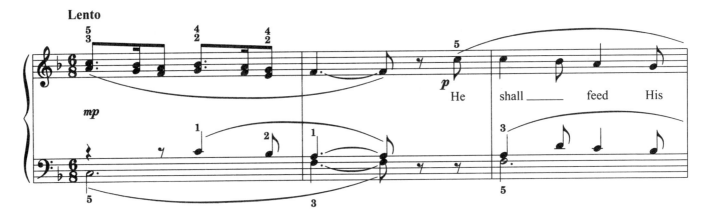

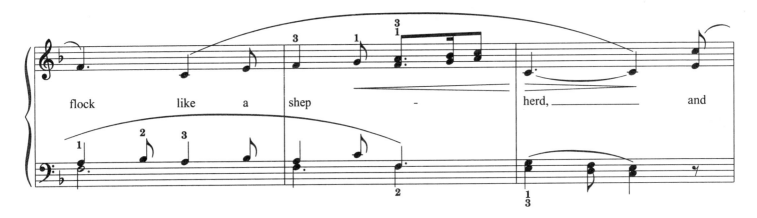

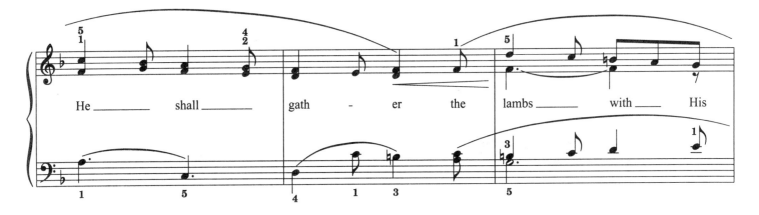

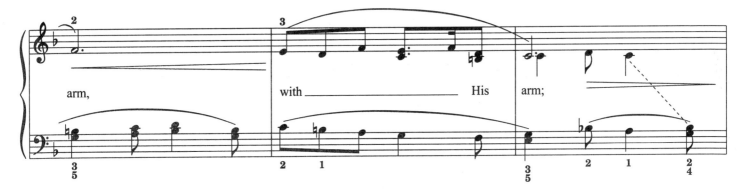

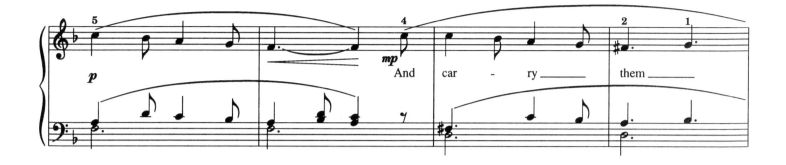

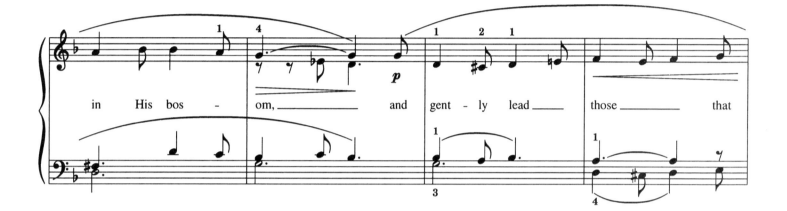

Behold the Lamb of God

from "Messiah"

Arr. by Frank Metis

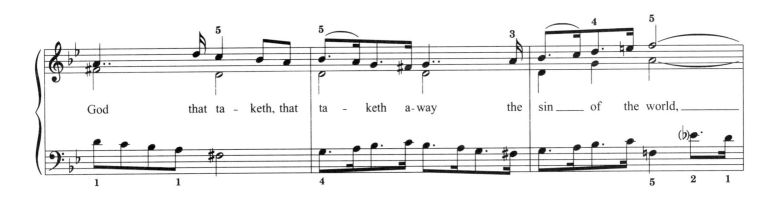

Why Do the Nations

from "Messiah"

Arr. by Frank Metis

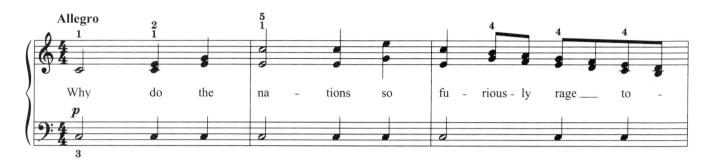

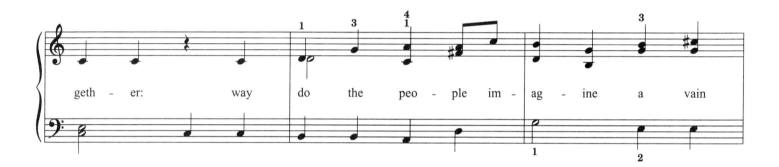

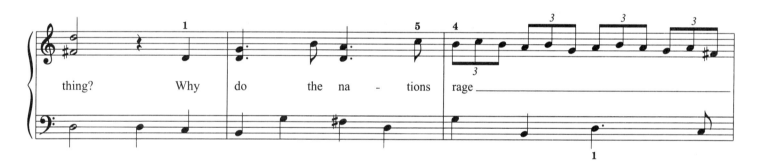

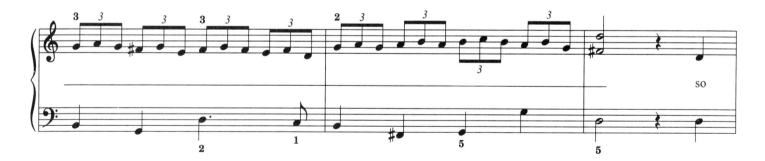

do the peo - ple im - ag - - - -

- - - - gine ___ a ___ vain ___

thing? im - ag - - - ine ___ a vain

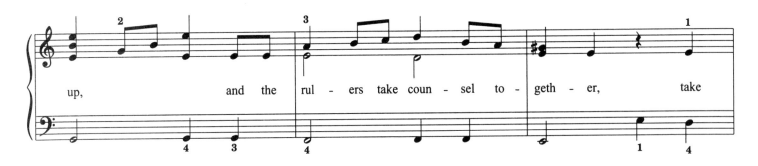

thing? The kings of the earth rise

up, and the rul - ers take coun - sel to - geth - er, take

coun - - -

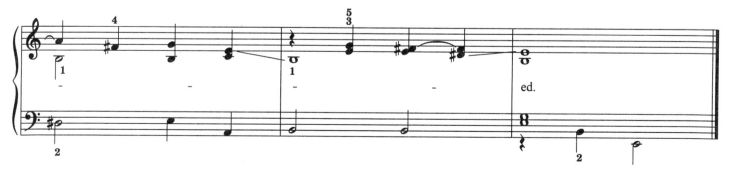

Thou Art Gone Up on High

from "Messiah"

Arr. by Frank Metis

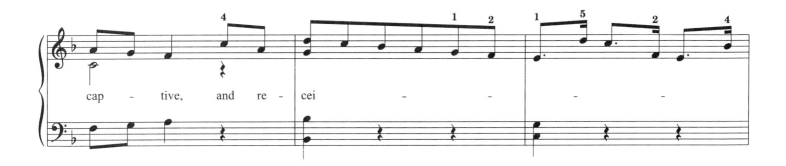

cap - tive, and re - cei

- - - - ved gifts _____ for _____

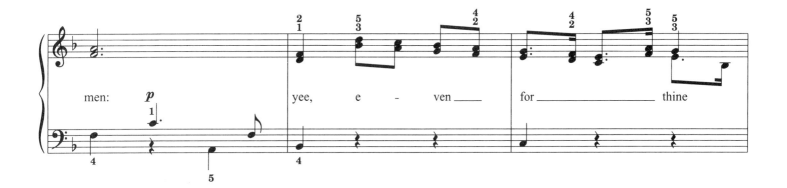

men: *p* yee, e - ven _____ for _____ thine

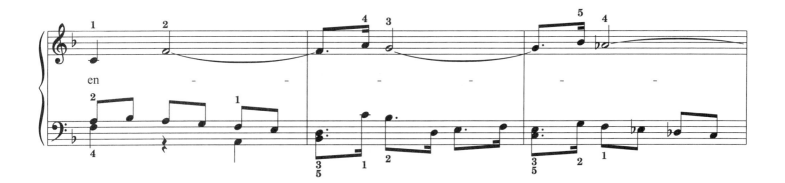

en - - - - - -

- - e - mies, yea, e - ven for ____

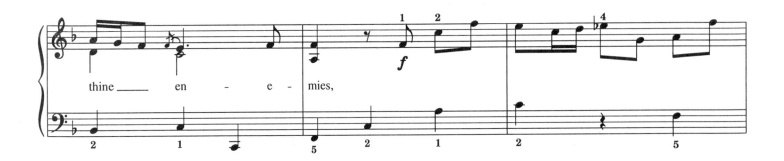

thine _____ en - e - mies,

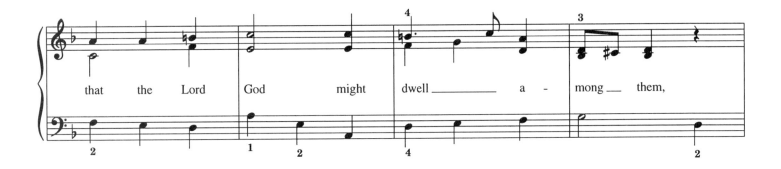

that the Lord God might dwell _____ a - mong __ them,

that the Lord, the Lord __ God might _____ dwell _____

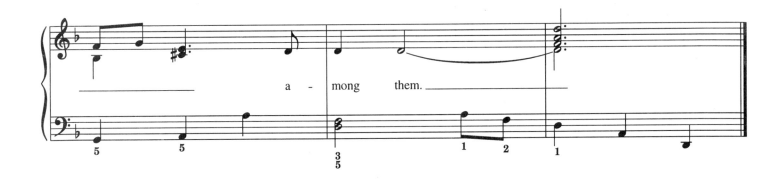

_____ a - mong them. _____

The Trumpet Shall Sound

from "Messiah"

Arr. by Denes Agay

sound, and the dead shall ___ be ___

raised, And the dead shall be

raised _____ in - cor - rup - ti - ble,

The trum - pet ___ shall sound

and ___ the ___ dead ___ shall ___ be ___ raised be

raised __ in - cor - rup - ti - ble,   and   we   shall   be

changed _____

_____   and   we   shall   be

changed,   we   shall   be ____ changed, _____

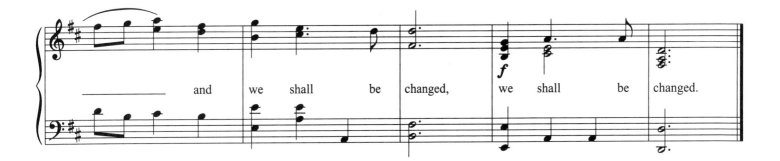

_____   and   we   shall   be   changed,   we   shall   be   changed.

How Beautiful Are the Feet

from "Messiah"

Arr. by Frank Metis

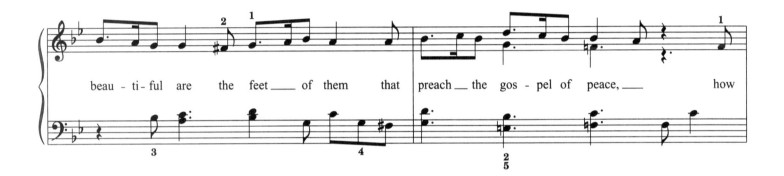

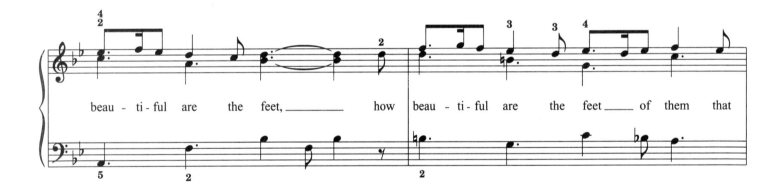

beau - ti - ful are the feet ___ of them that preach ___ the gos - pel of peace, and

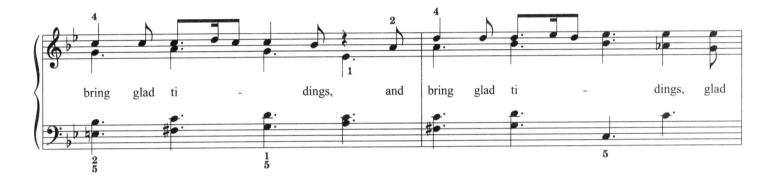

bring glad ti - dings, and bring glad ti - dings, glad

ti - dings of good things, and bring glad ti - dings, glad

ti - dings of good things, and bring _____ glad ti - dings, glad

ti - dings of ___ good things, glad ti - dings of _____ good things!

Behold and See

from "Messiah"

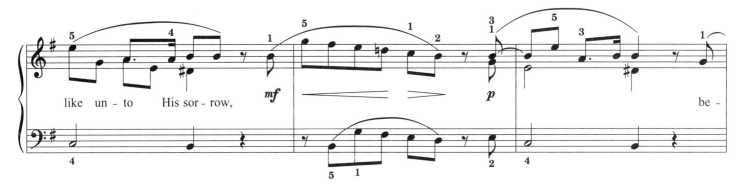

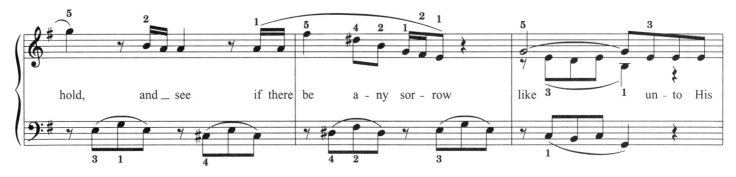

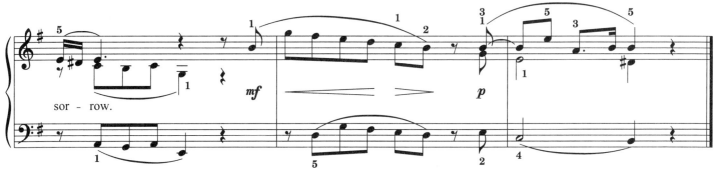

I Know that My Redeemer Liveth

from "Messiah"

Arr. by Denes Agay

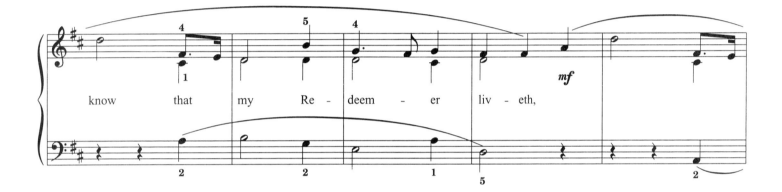

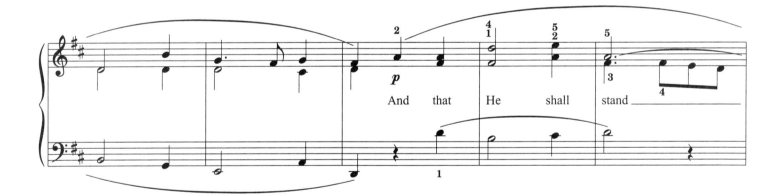

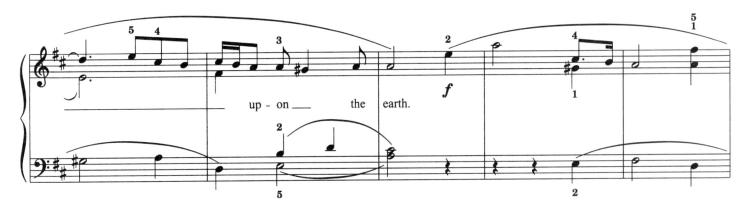

up - on ____ the earth.

I know that ____ my Re - deem - er

liv - eth, and that He shall ____ stand ____

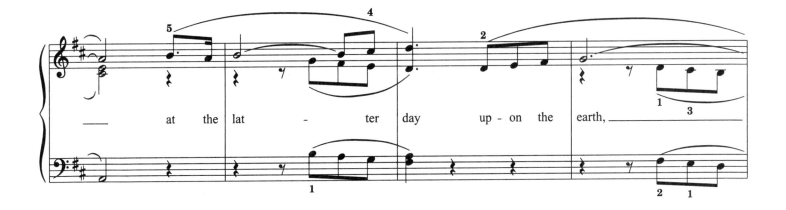

____ at the lat - ter day up - on the earth, ____

up - on the earth. I know

that my Re - deem - er liv - eth, and that He shall

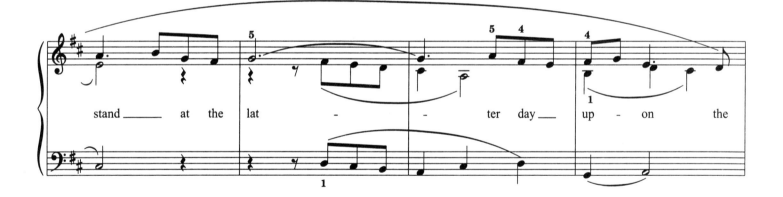

stand at the lat - ter day up - on the

earth, up - on the earth.

Hallelujah

from "Messiah"

Arr. by Frank Metis

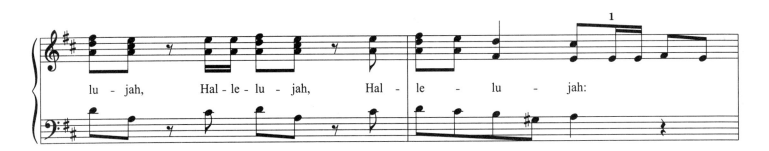

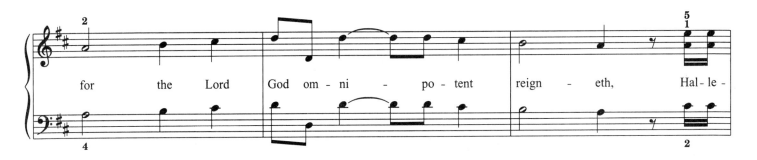

lu - jah, Hal - le - lu - jah, Hal - le - lu - jah, Hal - le - lu - jah:

for the Lord God om - ni - po - tent reign - eth, Hal - le -

lu - jah, Hal - le - lu - jah, Hal - le - lu - jah, Hal - le - lu - jah,

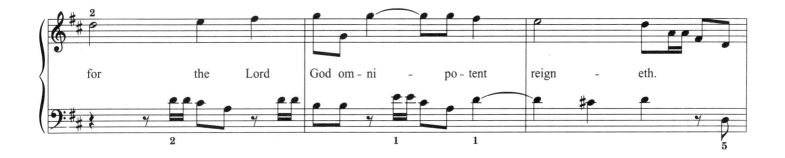

for the Lord God om - ni - po - tent reign - eth.

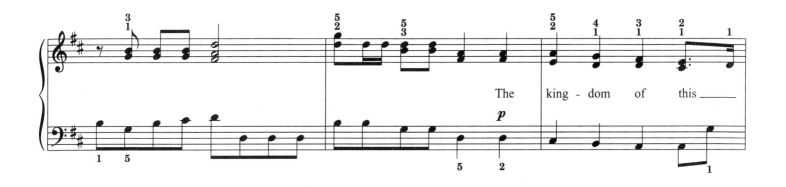

The king - dom of this_____

p

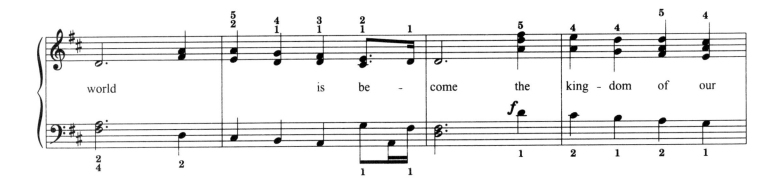

world   is be - come the king - dom of our

Lord   and of his Christ, and of his Christ; and he shall

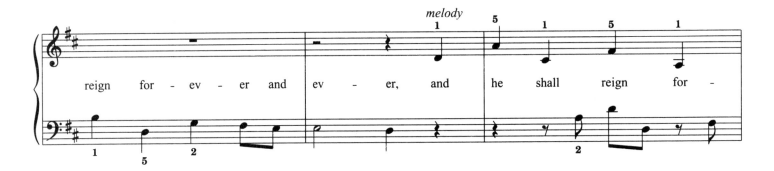

reign for - ev - er and ev - er, and he shall reign for -

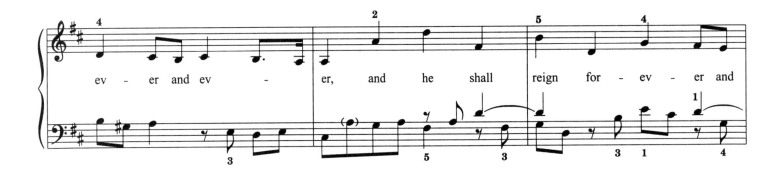

ev - er and ev - er, and he shall reign for - ev - er and

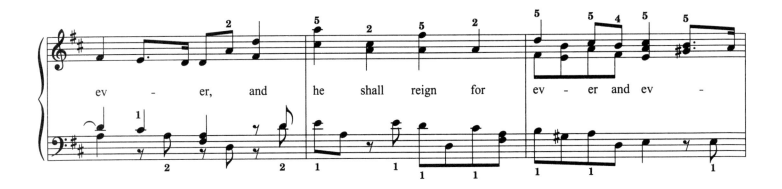

ev - er, and he shall reign for ev - er and ev -

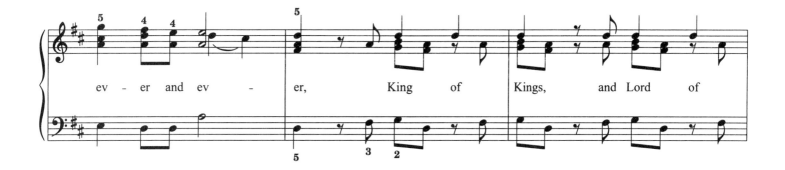

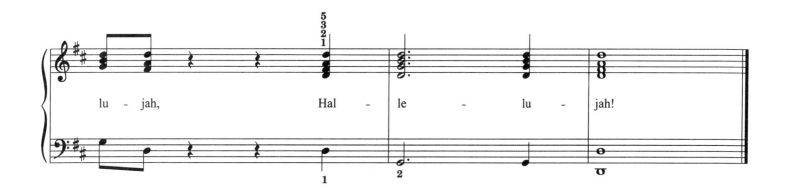

Where'er You Walk

from the oratorio "Semele"

Arr. by Denes Agay

Wher - e'er you walk, cool gales shall fan the ___

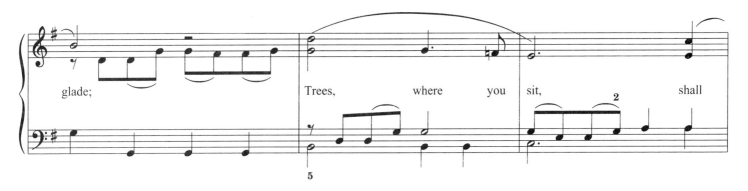

glade; Trees, where you sit, shall

crowd in - to a ___ shade,

Trees, where you ___ sit, shall crowd ___ in -

to ___ a shade.

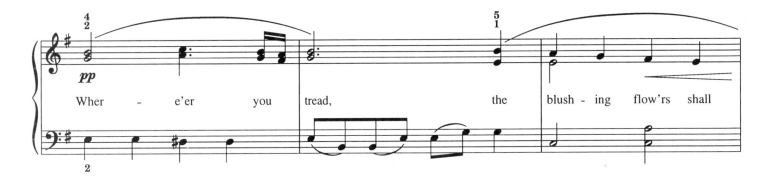

Wher - e'er you tread, the blush - ing flow'rs shall

rise, And all *cresc.* things flour - ish, and

all things flour - ish wher - e'er you turn your eyes, Wher -

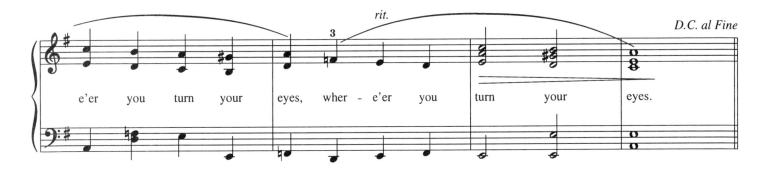

e'er you turn your eyes, wher - e'er you turn your eyes.

Love Ye the Lord

Largo *from* the opera "Xerxes"

Arr. by Denes Agay

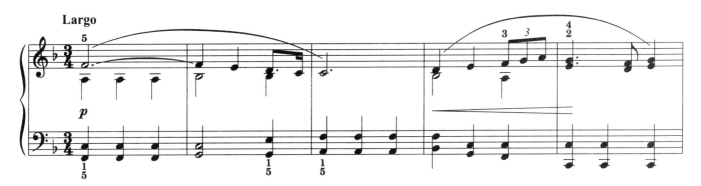

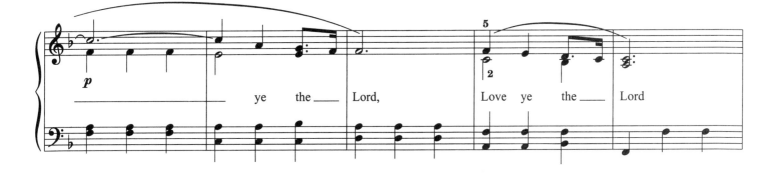

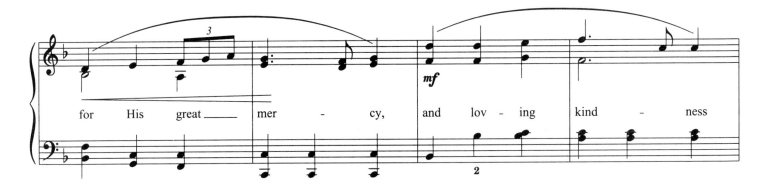

for His great _____ mer - cy, and lov - ing kind - ness

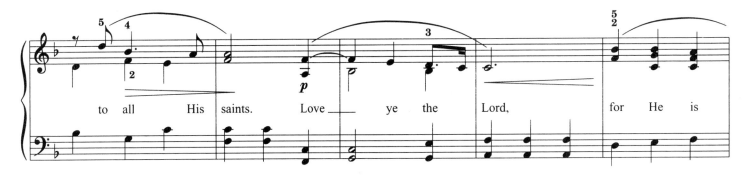

to all His saints. Love _____ ye the Lord, for He is

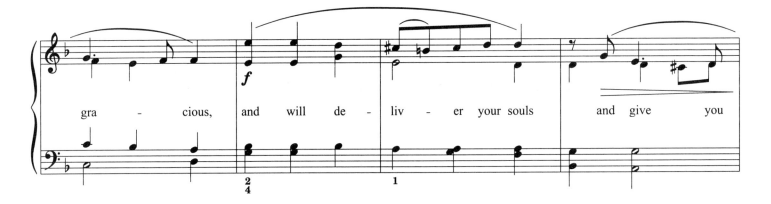

gra - cious, and will de - liv - er your souls and give you

peace. For _____ His ___ great mer - cy love ___ ye the ___ Lord, and

He will de - liv - er _____ you from all fear, and give _____ you

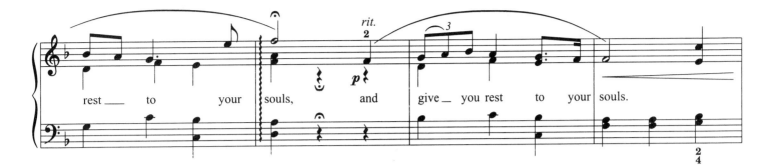

rest ___ to your souls, and give ___ you rest to your souls.

Air from Suite No. 5
"The Harmonious Blacksmith"

Hornpipe

from "Water Music"

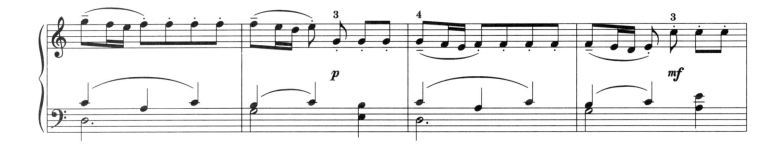

Air

from "Water Music"

Arr. by Denes Agay

See, the Conquering Hero Comes

from "Judas Maccabeus"

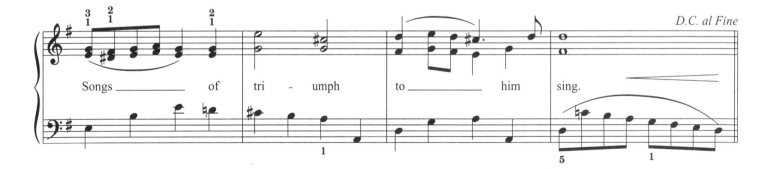